Plant the Seed Well...
Expect Wonders

A Parent's Guide to making sense of parenting in the 21st century

Written by Nury Castillo Crawford

Expect Wonders

Copyright 2019 by 1010 Publishing LLC

All rights reserved. Without limiting the rights under copyright reserved above, no part of this publication may be reproduced, stored in or introduced into a retrieval system, or transmitted, in any form or by any means (electronic, mechanical, photocopying, recording, or otherwise), without the prior written permission of both the copyright owner and the above publisher of this book. The scanning, uploading, and distribution of this book via the internet or via any other means without the permission of the publisher is illegal and punishable by law. Please purchase only authorized electronic editions and do not participate in or encourage electronic piracy of copyrighted materials. Your support of the author's rights is appreciated.

For information about permission to reproduce selections from this book, email 1010PublishingUS@gmail.com, subject line, "Permission".

www.1010publishing.com

ISBN 978-0-9993978-2-4

Printed in the United States of America.

Written by Nury Castillo Crawford

Plant the Seed Well...

Dedication

My greatest honor is the title of mother and my greatest treasure is my children. I have always considered them my life's biggest investment. My sons: Javier, Duane, and Marcos taught me consistently and repeatedly what unconditional love truly is. I did not have a step-by-step instructional book on how to be a good mother, but I was inspired daily by each of them to do the best I could.

Expect Wonders

My sweet loving mother, whose love I could never repay, left this earth in 2012, she will forever live in my heart and soul.

Here are some thoughts I have written to remember her:

Mi Mami

My guiding star.

My confidant.

My cheerleader.

My protector.

My role model.

The one I could always depend on... You taught me what true love is. I know I am blessed to have had the opportunity to share your space on earth. I miss you every single day of my life. I am living, but part of my heart will always be missing.

Your gentle love and support made me who I am today.

Written by Nury Castillo Crawford

Plant the Seed Well...

A Note from the Author

All of the advice, stories, and information are true to the best of my recollection and knowledge. This entire book is based on both personal and professional experiences. Names, personal experiences, and events have been changed to protect the privacy of friends, colleagues, professional contacts, family members, and acquaintances. If entire names are noted which included first and last names, then please know that name is not altered. Any resulting resemblance to other persons, living or dead, is coincidental and ultimately unintentional.

Contents

Dedication	4
A Note from the Author	6
Foreword	8
Acknowledgement	10
Preface	11
Introduction	15
There's Nothing Quite Like A Mother's Love:	18
Children Aren't Just Financially Expensive, Time Is The Real Struggle!	37
Choose Your Battles	46
Confidence	51
Knowledge Is Power:	58
You Have Rights	64
Let Them Fly On Their Own	72
Dedication	77
Advice for New Parents	78
Appendix	86

Written by Nury Castillo Crawford

Foreword

As educators, our focus is to ensure that all students realize their potential and take advantage of the opportunities offered in this country. As Latino educators, we not only focus on the education of students but also on the education of Latino families. While I was reading the book Plant the Seed Well ... Expect Wonders, I realized that Nury Crawford and I shared the same memories of our mothers. We share the same customs, advice and ideals. As Latino educators, we both see the importance of Latino parent participation in schools. We are who we are thanks to the involvement of our parents in the school. Although our mothers spoke only Spanish, not knowing the language was not an excuse for them to ignore our studies.

Today as mothers and educators we know that every child needs a positive influence in life, a motivating word and a loving smile, but support in the academic areas is essential to ensure a successful future in the life of your child. I assure you that if you follow the steps in this guide you will improve your skills as a parent of a child in the 21st century. We live in an era that is rapidly changing and we have to make sure our children are prepared and educated. This book is written in a style that is easy to understand and follow. The chapters in this book will help you to be a positive influence, not only in your home, but in the community.

Pilar Silva,

Middle School Teacher,

Forever Mother of a Beautiful Daughter

Plant the Seed Well...

Acknowledgement

A special thank you to my sister Ketty, my best friend. Thank you for always cheering me on and believing in me. We have literally have been together through it all.

To Earl, thanks for all of the great co-parenting and for supporting my strategies on how to raise our boys. I am not perfect (well mostly), but together we made a perfect parenting team.

Last but not least, to my three "cubs"- Javier, Duane and Marcos. I love each of you more than you could ever imagine. You are my everything. You made my role as a mother the best job ever!

I wouldn't change anything about you. I pray you continue to grow. Remember that when you fall down to quickly get back up. Never allow anyone to determine your potential.

Preface

Well if you've picked up this book, I assume you're interested in tips on how to navigate this thing called parenting. Twenty-five years of parenting has been an entire lifetime of learning for me. As the boys grew, I had many friends and family encourage me to write about my experiences with the boys. I would have started long ago, but I will be honest the biggest obstacle was time. When the boys were younger, all I wanted to do if I had time was sleep. Between a full-time job, three boys, a husband, dinners, laundry, and laundry (yes laundry gets a double honorable mention) … yeah…sleep.

I am an educator by profession. During my tenure at the elementary school level, I had many opportunities to advise parents and colleagues. I have kept a close relationship with many families. One of the various roles I have held in the public education systems was Parent Involvement Coordinator. I led the school's initiative to increase parental involvement with volunteering opportunities, mentoring activities, event attendance, workshop participation, and parent conferences. During these engagement opportunities, I was able to help parents gain knowledge of their rights in school, share the importance of structure, love and discipline with children, and the research that proves parent involvement equals positive results for both children and parents.

I can honestly say that writing the book was healing to me. Everything I share is from both personal and professional experiences. I've included a section of advice from other parents that I'm connected with on social media.

If I had to thank one person in particular, it would have to be my mom. She was a true reflection of what unselfish love looks like. My mom was a blend of high moral expectations and loyalty. She expected my siblings and me to make decisions that did not hurt anyone else or self, but also would stand by our side if we happened to make the wrong one. She would make sure we never felt like a mistake was the ultimate outcome of our lives. She believed in falling down and getting back up. She also believed in lending a helping hand to anyone, without thinking for a second if there was something in it for her just because she helped someone.

I started writing this book in the summer of 2016. I still work full-time so I wrote a little here and there, as time permitted (and if sleep didn't get in the way…ha ha ha). During this time I was sidetracked and ultimately wrote a bilingual, children's book entitled, "3,585 MILES TO BE AN AMERICAN GIRL". A story inspired by my personal journey to the USA as a child.

I hope that my stories and information will help you as you encounter the ultimate responsibility of your life. The purpose is to reiterate and support the decisions you have already made and possibly share new strategies and information you might find helpful in this journey we call parenthood.

Do you remember any lessons you might have learned from your mom? Like, remember to dance in the rain or wait thirty minutes after eating before going swimming? Most of the lessons I learned from my mother were in the context of being unselfish and owning up to my mistakes. This book starts with lessons that I learned from my mother, beginning with an important lesson about children having no control when they are conceived or whom they are born to. Children do not ask to come to this world. One of those lessons I am obedient to on a consistent basis, is that cooking does not have to be fancy it just has to be made with love. On a normal day to day, I cooked a healthy dinner. It was important to me to know that I provided healthy, home cooked meals for my sons. Throughout the writing of this book, I was able to engage with social media friends and asked them what advice they would give to new parents. I have embedded those responses in the book too.

Further, into the book, chapters are focused on additional advice and information you will find useful, from the most expensive cost to parents is not monetary but time and how as parents we have to learn to choose our battles and focus on the end game.

Introduction

I am the daughter of a beautiful couple, who grew up on a marginally low to a middle socioeconomic status household but don't tell my younger self that because she thought she was rich beyond means. Waking up having breakfast with both parents and siblings, coming home from school to a welcoming mother (and after-school snacks!), eating dinner and watching television as a family on a continual nightly basis. As an adult, I've slowly learned that foundation is everything. I am thankful for both of my parents, but as anyone would venture to guess, my role model of what a mother should be would ultimately be a reflection of my mom.

And so it begins, my journey into being a wife and into motherhood started when I was in my early 20s, still a student in my beloved Alma Mater, Florida A & M University in Tallahassee, Florida. I gave birth to Javier, the child who changed my life and helped me grow up, I am certain in record time. Half a decade pass by and I gave birth to my second son, my sweet, loving Duane, you will learn more about him in the book, and completed my Master's Program in a relatively close time frame of each other. Then as luck and destiny would have it, unexpectedly I am blessed with my last son, Marcos.

Let me tell you how my journey into writing this book began…

This book is a little bit about parenting from my perspective, with a few sprinkles of advice from other moms I personally know with a dash or two of the pertinent information you should know, see the section about Parents Rights.

I really hope you are able to find new information, receive affirmation of what you are doing as a mom or even find laughter on the things moms have to endure. In the end, a mom's love is incomparable to anything else I've ever witnessed. The title comes with no prior experience required and no one provides a how-to-model. A simple quote I have kept dear to my heart in moving forward with my own children is, "A mother's love is a reflection of God's love" Isaiah 66:13. It is my hope that this book is a part of your own how-to-model for your daily life with your child, it's a tough job so a mom has to do it! "A mother's love for her child is like nothing else in the world. It knows no law, no pity, it dates all things and crushes down remorselessly all that stands in its path." by Agatha Christie,

Plant the Seed Well… Expect Wonders

Love-

Nury

Plant the Seed Well…

There's Nothing Quite Like A Mother's Love:
Lessons I Learned From My Mother

In this chapter, we will venture into:

- Lessons that might actually hurt parents to make, but because the love for their child is stronger, parents will have to stand strong with resolve.

- Lessons that are not only applicable to the moment but teaches life-long character traits.

- Lessons that support children in having positive relationships with siblings, peers, parents, and even educators.

The lessons I learned from my mother are countless, but the ones that consistently stick out to me are the ones that I seem to run into, consciously or not, on a daily basis. The lessons encompass learned opportunities from relationships between mother and child as well as messages about hard decisions about your child.

Lesson 1- Children do not ask to come to this world. So whether or not you planned, were ready or not, for a new life to join yours, it has nothing to do with what your child needs or deserves. Never mind if you weren't thinking about a baby when you were intimate with your significant partner (referencing my own first experience). You are a parent. The influence and impact you have on your child are immeasurable. A bad school teacher can ruin a child for an average of four years, but a "bad" parent can ruin a child for life.

> *"Be involved, actively listen, be the parent...not their friend and have fun because this is the best role u will ever have!"*
>
> **Alicia – a mom of three, on Facebook**

I had a heart-wrenching conversation with a high school classmate. She is now a successful nurse, but after I shared a positive reflection about my own mother, she shared a private story that depicted the relationship she had with her own mother. She told me how her mother's boyfriend sexually assaulted her while we were in high school. When she reluctantly told her mother, her mother called her a liar and told her she was trying to ruin her relationship with her boyfriend. I cannot imagine such a scenario, where your own mother would question your intention. Ultimately, my high school peer ran away. Thankfully, she found herself on her own, but the hurt her mother bestowed upon her is still evident, 30 years later.

Lesson 2- You are not your child's friend. Children thrive off of structure…Yes- even those turbulent teenage years (which come along faster than ever anticipated), children need structure. They need to innately feel like someone is in control. That someone cannot be him/her. By no means am I trying to articulate that you can't have fun with your child, or love on your child every chance you get (I actually think that's important too!). It just means that when you know better- whether it's providing a glass of water versus a 20 oz. carbonated soda for lunch or allowing him/her to dictate a bedtime. You are the parent, you know better. You know excess calories impact weight, cause cavities, increase chances for diabetes, and so forth. Even if you like it too, you know it is your job to share that knowledge with your child. I have countless stories about parents trying to be their child's friend. Some of the reasons come from the guilt of a failed relationship with the father. Other times it comes from confusing the "choose your battles wisely" rule. I can quickly recall a situation where a young student about 7 years old, had a medical plan due to his diabetes and obesity. During the medical plan meeting, the teacher shared that the student bought ice cream daily from the school cafeteria and always had a family size package of chips. The teacher wanted to make sure the mother was aware. I was shocked and so was the certified nurse who was also attending the meeting. She asked the mother why the student would be allowed to have those type of foods daily. The mother said that if the child did not have access to it, there would be many behavior problems at home. That was the reason she had to send money for ice cream and purchase large size snacks. Of course, it was not my place to judge. I'm sure some of my dietary choices have not always been up to par, but I was appalled by the reasoning behind it. I wanted to say, if you don't buy it your child won't eat it. If you don't send the money for ice cream, your child might be upset, but not forever. This is a prime example of a parent trying not to upset their child, and therefore just doing what the child demands. Children don't need parents to be their friends. They need us to make adult, responsible decisions even when they are not the popular choice.

Lesson 3- Never say never when you have kids. Have you ever been out shopping or at a restaurant with a friend or your spouse when you notice a 3-year-old climbing the seats at the restaurant or running through the aisles of a busy grocery store without a care in the world? You might be quick to think your child would never do that but I can almost guarantee that the moment you think about making such a declaration you wild will prove you wrong.

I recall an instance when we went to my mom's bible study on a particular Wednesday at her friend's house. While we kids hung out in one of the back bedrooms, the moms held their bible study. We overheard one of the moms share that her unwed college daughter had become pregnant. As kids, we just looked at each other and kept playing. After the mom who shared the news left, the remaining ladies started to make condescending remarks about lack of self-respect and not having control over your own kids. There was a pause, and then I heard my mom speak up. She said that it could be any of their daughters and that it's never safe to say never when you have kids. That evening as we drove home, my mom looked at me (knowing I had overheard) and said, "Never throw stones in glass houses." I knew what she meant. Until this day, when I see moms having challenges with their kids, I always remember my mom's words to her friends and to me, on our way home. Kids are unpredictable and free will is always reflected in the decisions we all make. Just when you say not my kid is precisely when they will prove you wrong.

Lesson 4- Be empathetic. Giving is always better than receiving. That's an old saying, kind of cliché. It's actually true. As I've matured I've learned the importance of this lesson. Children learn more from actions than words. It is important for our children to see us being empathetic and caring towards others. My mom lived this lesson. I recall an early memory at a local grocery store. We were checking out. There was a young mother and her two young children, who were quite unhappy about a small, red vending machine that was full of those little cheap, plastic toys- bouncy balls, sticky bugs, etc. They wanted a toy. Their mom told them she did not have the money for toys. My mom went over and handed each of them one quarter, the mom smiled and told the boys to say thank you. They did as they swiftly ran towards the vending machine. This was not an isolated incident and it did not always end well for my mom, but she never allowed it to change her stance. Sometimes the moms literally told her to mind her own business. I would be outraged and would tell my mom not do that anymore, but as I mentioned earlier she didn't listen. Growing up, at some time or another we "hosted" more individuals and families, yes entire families, at our house than I would like to share. I recall my dad not loving it and me hating it. It meant I had to share everything! Did I already tell you that we were always low to middle class in terms of social economic status? Some of these scenarios end horribly. One time a neighbor and her kids were evicted from the house they were renting down the street, when we lived in Columbus, Indiana. My mom felt bad for them and invited her and her four – yes four- kids to move in. During that time, we were preparing to move to Florida and my mom told them they could rent our home once we left. She said they could live with us for that last month and a half. Well, that was a crazy month and a half in a three-bedroom house located in rural Indiana. When we finally moved, we left them almost everything. My parents planned with our neighbors and we would return and pick up the rest of our furniture, washer, dryer, etc. When we returned a month later everything was gone, including the family. To top it off, they busted windows, and the place smelled like dead raccoons. Actually, I don't know what dead raccoons smell like but I think it would be equivalent to that stench. If my mom cursed then, I'll never know. She did not in front of me. She only cried and said they must have been in serious trouble.

One of mom's most notable quote was, "As bien sin mirar aquien", although there is no direct translation, its context can be interpreted as, "Do right without expecting anything in return". As a child, this was very impactful to me and a lesson I will never forget. I feel like I live this more than I notice myself. Growing up I did not like it at all, but as an adult, I understand it and understand why my mom was so giving.

Lesson 5- Give love to everyone. One of the saddest moments for me is having talked to kids, from elementary age to high school age, about why they called a peer a degrading term, racial, gender bashing or social economic status insults. I recall the message President Obama, USA President 44 tweeted after the Charlottesville White supremacist protest: "No one is born hating another person". As adults we all need to self-reflect and make sure we do not pass down ill feelings about other people to our own kids, we want them to be better versions of ourselves, right?

I deeply loved my mom ever since I can recall. I loved to watch her cook. I loved to walk anywhere holding hands and spend time watching Bonanza, a telenovela, or whatever it was she wanted to watch. Any chance I could muster to acquire a one on one was probably my most prized possession as a young girl. All of that to say, I was not always willing to share her if I had any say so. I know, it sounds selfish, but it is true. My mom knew I told her how I felt, but she reminded me that everyone needed love. That I should not let my heart be selfish. That being nice was important. One example where she showed me to love others was a day where a young boy who was a neighbor down the street happened to stop by before school. My mom asked him what he was doing. He said it was his birthday, but his mom would be at work during the evening shift.

He continued to tell us that he wouldn't even get a cake. After he left, my mom began to make a homemade cake. Not just any cake. It was a torta helada, a very complicated recipe from scratch which included layers of orange gelatin and homemade whipped cream. When the buses unloaded that afternoon, she walked down the street to his house with this enormous cake! She rang the doorbell, walked in and handed him his cake. His mom was not home, and his stepfather was speechless. As my mom walked out, his stepdad asked my mom why she made the cake, and she said because it was a special day. This reiterated to me how important it was to be loving to everyone, regardless of what they could do for you.

Lesson 6- Family first. Whether your family consists of a traditional two-parent household, mom, and dad or mom and grandma or even a single parent, a family is the single most important influence in your child's life, and your child's first glace and experience with relationships. From their first moments of life, children depend on their family to protect them and provide for their needs.

Although this lesson might seem like common sense, it actually isn't. Based on all we hear about in the current events news, I think it's one of those lessons we should all heed. Once a woman has a child, she becomes a mom first and foremost. That her position at work or to her husband (or significant other) becomes secondary. It does not mean to neglect your responsibilities in any other role, it just means that whatever decision you make whether at work or in a personal relationship you should always think about the outcome for your child. Whether you are invited to an adult gathering and cannot take your child or if there is a difference in discipline measures between you and your significant other. You should always think, how does this impact my child?

I remember once when I had a huge argument with my dad (darn those teenage years!). My dad was, and still is, very old school in terms of rules and parameters for his daughters (not so much for my brother). I had a high school boyfriend and went out one evening. I was less than ten minutes late due to traffic. We didn't have cell phones then so I couldn't alert my dad that I was on the way. When I got home, he grounded me for a month and wouldn't allow me to explain. I became upset and told him he was unjust and mean. He became very angry and told me to shut up or leave. So I shrugged my shoulders, wiped my tears and proceeded to go to my room to pack. I overheard my mom tell him that if I left she would leave too, that he needed to calm down and talk to me later about my consequence. I walked out in time to see him turn around and go into their bedroom. My mom told me to take a shower, and that it would continue the next day. Although I was ultimately still grounded, my dad did talk to me and allowed me to tell my side of the story. He made sure I understood I could not be late, not even ten minutes and for that I thank him. That evening, I felt my mom's true love and felt she would always have my back, which she has proved time and time again.

Lesson 7- Don't hold grudges. We often hear that holding grudges is bad for you. According to WebMD, it is unhealthy. People that don't forgive can reflect faster heart rates, higher blood pressures, and more distressed facial gestures when asked about the unpleasant incident. Forgiving is something I have had to work on. I'm not as forgiving as I need to be, so I'm a work in progress. One flashback that comes immediately to mind, is the relationship my mom had

Plant the Seed Well…

with her sisters; not necessarily her siblings, just her sisters. My mom was somewhere in the middle chronologically of her line of siblings. All in all, there were about twelve of them. So I believe all of the backstabbing and jealousy type behaviors came from fighting for their own mom's attention. They grew up with very little means. I can honestly say that half of their interactions ended up with someone saying something mean and making my mom cry. Sometimes those mean things were directed at her and other times not. Nevertheless, it hurt my mom's feelings. She loved her family. As I grew up and was exposed to this toxic relationship with most of her siblings, I resented all of them I knew hurt her. Every chance that I had I encouraged my mom to walk away from them. I tried to convince her that it was not healthy for her to be around them. Each and every single time she forgave them. I could not understand it then. Even now I have a hard time understanding it in its totality. My mom would tell me that she could not just walk away from her siblings. She forgave them because she loved them. I believe this helped her to be happy.

Lesson 8- Cooking doesn't have to be fancy, it just has to be made with love. 90% of the time I still cook dinner. I have a full-time profession, but since I was not raised on fast food or eating out I am compelled to have a homemade meal each evening if at all possible. I will admit that there were nights here and there where I picked up dinner or ordered a pizza. Those nights were not common, but really late nights at work make those compromises almost inevitable. My mom cooked dinner every single night. She said it had to be made with lots of love. I guess by love, she meant it had to taste really, really good. We are from Hispanic/Latino descent, South America to be more accurate, and Peru to be precise. My mom was a walking cookbook and possessed culinary gifts known to anyone who ever had any dish prepared by her, whether it was an appetizer, a main course or dessert… even her salads were delicious! In 2015, World Travel Magazine named Peru as the Culinary Destination of the world. When this was noted as public information, I immediately aligned it with my mom. Thinking, "Yep, no wonder!" Each one of us is born with a grandeur gift and some of us spend our entire life trying to figure out what it is, I believe my mom learned what hers was by the time she was 15 years old. She cooked every night, though I believe we might have had leftovers, my dad was not a fan of that. He liked fresh food daily. Even if we had a basic tomato based sauce spaghetti, she would shred the carrots, fry them up with garlic and onions, and add the tomato sauce. She would add her secret ingredient, oregano, a couple basil leaves and violà! Served over pasta and I could eat three bowls! From a chicken tamale and toast for breakfast to a surprise homemade apple pie on any given night, mom seemed to be at her best in the kitchen. It brought all of us to the table, where we laughed, talked, argued, discussed issues, and just spent time together. This is where my parents would hear how school was or when I would ask if I could visit a friend after school. I laugh now thinking about how much she fed us, I'm surprised I didn't grow up with obesity issues. That conversation is for another time.

Lesson 9- Enjoy your childhood. Children grow up way faster than we ever anticipated. No, it does not initially feel or seem that way. They need you for everything from feeding them to bathing them. When I became a mother for the first time, there were times I wanted or felt I needed a break. My mom would tell me to remember that each day my baby would need me less and less. Those words quickly came to fruition. I learned that lesson quickly with my firstborn. He learned to walk and talk, feed himself, get his own toys out of the toy chest, etc. So I quickly learned to enjoy the boys' childhood. I spent a lot of time playing with them, reading to them, talking to them, teaching them, basic things like counting while cooking or cleaning up.

I recall a conversation with my oldest, he was in middle school, he came home. I was washing dishes and asked him how his day went. Like most kids, his immediate response was, "it was okay". I expected it, so I knew to ask specific questions. So I asked him if anything interesting happened. He shared that a girl asked him for a kiss behind the gymnasium. Instinctively I wanted to turn away from the sink, drop the dish on the ground and ask him her name so I could report it...but I didn't (that seems a little extreme now). I told him, "that is interesting" and then proceeded him to tell me what happened next. He said, "I told her to slow down and enjoy her childhood." I smiled in and out, "Good job son!"

Lesson 10- Children need their father. I've read reports and articles that show that if your child's father is affectionate, supportive, and involved, he can contribute greatly to your child's cognitive, language, and social development. Of course, this will be reflected in your child's social and academic achievement. Dads can play a vital role to daughters and sons. Dads can provide that strong inner core resource. Fathers can give their kids a sense of well-being, good self-esteem, and authenticity.

Regardless of your relationship with your child's father, kids need their dad. The Father Involvement Research Alliance notes that children with involved fathers perform better both socially and academically. Dads fill a space no one else can fill. In the long run, long-term relationships are bound to be more successful too. Girls look for those same characteristics in men for future relationships, whether they know it or not. I'm sure it would seem a lot easier to raise a child without someone else's opinion, perceptions, or feedback to consider. I know there were plenty of times where my view into a situation or instance was completely different than their dad's. Since I have always respected him as a father, I took a step back and looked at the bigger picture. I am a "mama bear" as some have called me, so that's not always so easy. I learned that if you want to see the entire elephant, you have to take a step back. Otherwise, if you stand too close, you won't see anything but dry, gray skin. All of that to say, that I had to learn to trust his point of view. I learned that I could not always see his perception, because he is a man and I am not.

Summary:

Lessons taught to our children are not always easy or fun. That's why they're called lessons. They have been known to hurt your feelings as a parent. Sometimes they might even make you feel a little guilty. Who really does not want their child to like them? Truthfully, I know I have always wanted to be liked by my own kids, but the goals I had for each of them to be contributing citizens of this planet we call earth have always been the bigger calling. It's always so much easier to judge what others are or are not doing with or for their own offspring. So it is imperative we all learn to be reflective. It is a must to be able to see the bigger picture. It is our duty to ensure our children grow and are exposed to experiences that are related to their age and maturity level. You are not their friend first. You are the parent first. So go ahead and check those social media posts. Make sure you have those mobile device passcodes. Learn their friends' names. Pop visits to the school are also okay. Contact their teachers via email or social media to check up on school events or your child.

Here is a tip!

Create a cheat sheet with your kids' social media usernames and passcodes. In addition, make sure you are connected with each of them on all social media platforms. You will be surprised how much you can learn from their posts.

Children Aren't Just Financially Expensive, Time Is The Real Struggle!

In this chapter we will venture into:

- The importance of time management whether you have one or three children.
- Making time for the little things.
- Actions speak louder than words. Make sure your actions tell your child that he/she is important.

One thing for sure is that when people start talking about having kids or even one-day having kids of their own, the first thing they say is, "Kids are so expensive!". For a while there, I must admit, I would readily concur. Sure it costs money to have children, from the prenatal care of doctor visits to the delivery itself. Even if you have health insurance, it costs money. Moms usually take off about six weeks from work. Never mind, if you come to work earlier than that. Your

> *"Spend as much time with your kids as possible."*
> Lisa – a mom on Facebook

co-workers will look at you like you've just won the Worst Mom Award. Then there's baby furniture, diapers, formula (if you're not breastfeeding), and of course who can forget childcare. Childcare costs just about as much as a car payments nowadays. Even though this is just the beginning of financial costs, it doesn't even come close to the amount of time it truly costs you. You see in terms of financial costs, if you are married or have a parent partner you can both pitch in, it can still cause hardships but it's doable. If you qualify for government subsidies, then that can help along the way too. But when it comes to time… money can't buy time. You see children aren't machines. You can't just set them on "go" or "pause" (although that would be pretty nice if you could). Well, in reality, you cannot. When they are newborn, it is understandable and you quickly learn that you have to do everything from feeding to clothing to bathing. The issue or misunderstanding comes in when they start walking or being able to play with toys or even watch a 30-minute show. This is when we can at times begin a trend of severe errors when it comes to our kids. We begin to assume that since they can sit down and be entertained by a TV show or a game on your tablet or phone, then it's okay to leave them. Sure it gives you a quick break, but what happens is that 1) you allow those 30 minutes to become two hours, 2) you don't find it necessary to communicate with your child about what he/she is watching. Even if the program is suited for your child's age, nothing and I mean absolutely nothing can replace the input, the background knowledge and feedback that you can as the parent. You see, programming even for children is just that programming. You don't want or need to allow anyone else besides the person who has a vested interest in your child to program him/her. I'm definitely not an extremist, but I find it very serious that we would allow our children to receive any type of media or information without our intervention. Children need to know that regardless of what is going on they are the priority. You see self-confidence has been repeatedly proven to be an impactful variable in the success of people. Our own children are our biggest investment. Their ultimate outcome is a reflection of us, their children and the love they receive from their parents, our kids, will reflect our impact on our own kids. Children learn more from actions versus what we tell them. We can spend an endless amount of hours telling them to read a book, but it is much more effective to have them see us reading. Reading to your kids at night before they go to bed is a great way to allow children to enjoy literature and watch you read. When you read to your child or children you allow them to hear inflection, discuss the book, ask questions, and guess what? If you have more than one child you can read to them together. Have the kids come to you on the couch or you can take turns in each of their rooms…Yep! Squeeze in a bed and read together…helps build bonds. As they get older and have to keep a reading log for school, you can take turns. You can break it down to one paragraph or one page at a time.

I recall busy Saturday mornings…three boys. Since I was and still am a full-time employee, weekends were spent with boys' activities and house chores. I would get started as early as possible on Saturday mornings, to try and get the most out of the day. As I cleaned up, I'd try and get the laundry in. I'd put on some classical music and get started. I heard as a young mother that classical music could make your babies smarter, so I just tried it just because. The boys would take turns following me around like ducklings follow their mother. In order to occupy them, I would set out Lego building blocks on the family room floor and pause to help build or ask a question about what they were building. Other times, one would follow me and ask me to read a book. I'd stop, wherever I was- whether it was on the middle of the stairs or on the hallway floor. Put him on my lap and open the book. I always loved when they asked me to read to them and I wanted them to love it too. Bath times were fun, there were always some toys in there, it's great to let children use their imagination. Early baths were always filled with singing the alphabet in English or Spanish or both! I also took the opportunity to teach it to them in sign language. Nowadays with access to the internet, you could basically teach your child just about anything. We all learn about 90% of everything we will learn in a lifetime between the ages of 0-5 years old. That's amazing, so the earlier you get started teaching and exposing your child to new experiences, the better for them.

I made posters with pictures and basic words and hung them around in the kitchen. I labeled basic things around the house and in their bedroom. For example, I would have a picture of me and next to it, it would say, "mom". Not 100 words, just five to ten words on the poster. In addition, as we would pass by the labeled door, I'd point to the word and say, "Oh that's the door".

There were children magazines, many I subscribed to but some definitely handed me downs or used ones from a second-hand store. The house had baskets of books in every single room. There were books and magazines on tables. I'd set up the hardcover ones like they were on display. During holidays such as Christmas, I'd have books about holidays and Christmas throughout the house. Throughout the year you could always find books about Hispanics and African Americans that made a historical impact on our country and the world. It is important that children can see themselves in positive books and movies. They need to be able to relate to the books they are exposed to. Does this mean they should never read books about other cultures and people? Of course not, the world is much larger than our own circles. Children (and adults) should always make an effort to read and celebrate other people as well.

As the children grew, they were signed up and registered to various sports, clubs, and activities. All of those things sound pretty awesome, right? Yeah, well that's where that little variable called time comes to play again. I recall when Javier started playing soccer at the age of four. That was actually, unbeknownst to my husband and I at the time, the easiest we were going to have it in terms of time management. Javier would have practice two times per week after school and a game each Saturday per season. So that would mean about two hours (before practice, practice, snack time, after practice) twice per week and two hours each Saturday. We were literally confined to the city limits and were pre-scheduled. We soon had an addition to our family, welcoming our second son. Soon enough he was involved in extracurricular activities. I think it was karate first, we had to take turns taking the boys to practice, in addition to making sure we had dinner ready. To add to our busy schedule, we welcomed our third and youngest son. He added a new challenge to us as parents, we had to make sure he didn't have to spend all of his time traveling each afternoon. Eventually, all three boys were in soccer, football, Boy Scouts, piano, after-school activities, and so on and so forth. There were evenings when a cooked meal at home did not happen. I have to confess we had more than a couple of nights of fast food during those years.

Summary:

Being able to map out your weekly schedule will help you and your child stay on task. Being organized helps you stay afloat and not feel so overwhelmed with life. It is not easy to manage another person's schedule into yours and it certainly feels almost surreal that you'd be able to do so if you have more than one child. The key to success with minimal stress is to be organized. Research says that if you write something down you're more likely to follow through with it because you're more likely to remember it…so go ahead and write down a daily and weekly schedule, which should include check your child's social media posts, include their practice times and game days, and even homework time.

Here is a tip!

Create a Google Calendar, which will be accessible on your mobile device and home computer. You can provide access to your family by sharing it with them. This way you are all in the loop! Communication is the key to success in any relationship.

Plant the Seed Well...

Choose Your Battles

In this chapter we will venture into:

- House rules and expectations should be realistic.
- Consequences should be aligned with the action.
- Too much of anything can ruin everything, this goes for the number of rules you have at home too.

> *"Take deep breaths, think before you speak cause words can leave scars too."*
> Jessica - a mom of two girls on Facebook

Thankfully unlike the Bermuda triangle where thousands of lives have not been lost... having children will make you feel like you are lost, but ultimately you are not. As naturally expected they will try to manipulate situations, push boundaries, and even challenge decisions you have made. In a black and white world, there is no gray area. Fortunately for us parents, we do not reside there. The world we live in as far as parent and children are concerned are full of gray areas. Don't misunderstand me, there are some rules that are steadfast and no means no; but at the same time there are some times when we call out an ultimatum and then find ourselves in an internal battle on how to stand by our "threat".

When used appropriately, rules provide a sense of predictability and consistency for children, thereby promoting physical and emotional safety. As parents, one should prioritize and establish a few rules that are the most important. The word "few" is a keyword. You cannot have so many rules that even you can't remember what they are. Plus it will help you and your child follow them with more consistency and perhaps not spend so much time policing the compliance part.

I remember a time I came up with this rule due to my frustration that my oldest, at the time in high school and highly involved in as many activities as he possibly could fit in a day, well the rule was when mom calls or texts you had to answer or reply within a thirty minute lapse. A Saturday came around, he left with his crew to hang out. Me, as a forever working on the Best Mom Around badge, I call to check on him. He doesn't answer, I leave a voicemail message and proceed to text him as well. The minutes move fast on the clock and I fear he won't make the thirty minute time frame. So I call again and it goes to voicemail again. Now I've worked myself up thinking how dare he doesn't answer while simultaneously beginning to worry with my own thoughts of all that could be going wrong. I attempt to wait patiently for what seems an eternity, by now thirty minutes have surely lapsed. I look at the clock and it is now about forty-five minutes. I call and leave a voicemail message, similar to "This is mom, I've tried to call and text you to no avail. If you don't call me back within thirty minutes from this message your phone privileges are revoked." Guess what happened? He didn't call. I went online to access the mobile phone account services and suspended it. A few minutes go by and I receive a call from an unknown number. It's my son, he tells me he's been in a soccer game and when he returned his phone was not working. I proceed to tell him the whole scenario. He tells me now that I know the reality, I should just turn his phone back on. At this point, I'm still upset so of course, I did not. He gets home and wants to discuss the consequence, but I am not interested. A couple of days lapse and I start to reflect…

is this necessary? He excels academically, has never been a behavior issue, and throughout all of this has remained his composure. Still, he didn't answer or respond within thirty minutes, that needs a consequence, right? Not that he ever was or is perfect without fault, but he had and has proven to be a thoughtful son. Two more days passed and then I had a talk with him. He desperately needed his phone services reinstated and I granted it. You see, it's okay to acknowledge when you've made a rash decision. The rule was an effective rule for the majority of the time, but this instance proved show there were exceptions.

It is okay to have a conversation with your child and let him or her know your thought process. Engaging your child in why a rule is in place and why a consequence is needed is a way of modeling for your child the reason parameters are set. I am not saying that your child will understand or agree with any of it, I'm just saying that it helps the relationship.

Summary:

A more effective way to get compliance to house rules and

expectations is to work on the list together. Working on the list together does not mean you only implement the rules your child wants or creates. Working on the list together simply means that you can learn more about your child in the process and your child can learn the importance of parameters. In society, the rules are called laws. Laws have higher consequences overall, so it is important to teach our children about parameters and expectations. Rules and consequences are not black and white or event right and wrong, there is a gray area. That is where communication plays an important role. Be open to listening, this will help the relationship you have with your child. Trust goes along with communication. Take every opportunity you have to affirm that relationship.

Here is a tip!

As you discuss the rules for the first time or just as a reminder, write them down and post them in the kitchen or room where everyone frequents. This will help serve as a reminder for everyone in the house and help you be consistent.

Confidence
Who gives it and how?

In this chapter, we will venture into:

- Tips on how to help your child build self-confidence.
- The importance of self-confidence.
- Your important role throughout your child's life in helping him/her believe that they can be successful.

The word confidence is derived from the Latin language root meaning "with trust, faith or belief". A confident child grows up to be a confident adult. Children who display confidence reflect a belief in his or her own abilities. The first step is to teach them to learn to trust to believe in themselves.

> *"Laugh and laugh often. Let them fail that is how they learn and build character."*
>
> **Debra –a mom on Facebook**

It has been noted that self-confidence can determine what you will achieve in life and can ultimately alter your level of happiness too.

Plant the Seed Well...

The doll test/ experiments during the 1940s by two African American psychologists brought forth some real-life data about perceptions children learn about themselves from their own experiences and environments. Kenneth and Mami Phipps presented results in The Brown vs. The Board of Education in 1954. In addition, they published three major papers between 1939 and 1940 on children's self-perception related to race. The doll experiment involved a preschool child being presented with two dolls. Both of these dolls were completely identical except for the skin and hair color. One doll was white with yellow hair, while the other was brown with black hair. It concluded that those African-American pre-school children assessed predominantly chose the white pictured doll as the "good" or "nice" doll more than not. Similar studies have stemmed from this original research. All have come to similar conclusions, that what children believe about themselves makes an impact on how they view the world. I learned about this experiment early in college so I kept in mind when I had my own children. I took as many opportunities as possible to impress on my own children their own positive attributes, leaving nothing to chance. I told each other them together or individually that I loved them. "Your skin tone is beautiful."; "Your hair texture is definitely perfect!" or "There's no one smarter than you."

Children need to see themselves in successful people that look like them, in situations that are not foreign to them. That's why it's important to expose them to different situations and environments. Children who are confident, trust their own abilities and thinking. Encouraging while listening to what your children have to share is an important variable in nurturing their self-confidence. One way to actively help children grow in this area is by encouraging them to take risks and allowing them to fail without feeling like a failure. Supporting them by providing those opportunities to try new things and helping them realize one can get better at things.

It's been noted time and time again that self-confidence can have a direct effect on children's success in school vs. their ability level. That's not to say that children's ability levels are not real since we know each one of us learns in different ways and at different rates, but believing that we can be successful in learning whatever the task

Plant the Seed Well...

is can make a world of difference. Children need to believe and be reassured that even if they have a challenge learning something that the teacher will help them learn and ultimately their parents will support them with whatever it is that they're struggling in.

Summary:

Instilling and helping our children acquire self-confidence might be a little more challenging than what you may think. The world outside your reach can be at times cruel. The influx of constant information which they can access on the world wide web in a second's notice is almost surreal. I suggest something that comes natural to parents, show your kids love. Be consistent in the love you share with them, help them set goals and be a role model for positive thinking and positive actions. Having a structured consistent home will help your child feel safe and ultimately help your child feel confident.

Here are some personal tips in helping your child build his /her self-confidence:

- LOVE your child- Do this the best way you

know how. Feeling accepted and being loved unconditionally is a huge variable. Guess what? If you make a mistake, admit it, say you are sorry…it's ultimately okay. Admitting to a mistake is part of a healthy relationship.

- Give kudos and high fives when it is warranted- Children need to know they all cannot be great at everything. If they succeed then yes a fist bump is needed otherwise just praise the effort.

- Mirror self-love- Yup! You've heard of that quote, "You can't love others until you love yourself"? It is true. Your child needs to see you rewarding yourself, taking care of yourself, physically, emotionally and mentally. Children will mimic more your actions versus what you tell them.

- Structure- Whether it is setting goals or following house rules, children need to learn how to envision the desired outcome (a goal) and how to go about to make sure the goal is met. When it comes to rules, children need to know the behavior expectations, the more consistent you are as a parent the more your child will build self-confidence. Enough where one day if peer pressure comes around (which it will), he/she will have the confidence to say, "no".

- Hobbies/Interests/Passion- If your child has an interest, scouting or min-marathons or even coding, make sure you genuinely pay attention and show your child with your actions that you too are interested. Show your child that you are interested not necessarily because you like it but more so because it is important to him/her.

Here is a tip!

Set aside some time each day. On average, parents spend about ten minutes talking to their child during four different time frames during the day which include breakfast, after school, dinner, and bedtime. I know most parents don't have dinner scheduled as "a family sit down" time, on a daily basis. That leaves most parents with three times per day. Therefore, on average most parents spend about 30 minutes a day talking with their child.

Our children are only young once. We have a small window of opportunity to spend time with them and to help guide them to become healthy, responsible young adults. So I suggest a family game night! The board game or game you choose to play is really not that big of a deal. The important part is to have a time set aside each week where you can talk, laugh and have some fun together. Building and maintaining a positive relationship takes time and it takes communication. You will be surprised about what you can learn during these times spent together.

Plant the Seed Well...

Knowledge Is Power: Know Where They Are And What They're Doing

In this chapter, we will venture into:

- The importance of knowing where your child is at all times.
- Communicating with your child.
- Making sure you know your child's friends.

"Parenting is learning when to Nurture, when to Mentor, and when to Coach."
Jerri –a mom of two, on Facebook

One of the hardest things to do is be everywhere your child is. It is a lot easier when they are babies, probably because they can't really move unless you move them…but it soon becomes a reality that you will not be able to keep up when they begin to crawl. Then they start walking, everyone is so excited and cannot believe how cute it is. Fast forward two weeks, now that cute little baby is everywhere and you cannot keep up. You have to shut doors and make sure cabinets have locks. All of this actually averages out to be easier than when they transform into those elementary school years. Sleepovers, birthday gatherings, outings with best friend's families, so on and so forth. Anything and everything can happen, with the moral stability of the world nowadays it doesn't bring any comfort to parents.

I immediately recall a story about a sleepover I wanted to attend. Let's see, I was probably about eleven years old. I attended a small parochial Catholic school in Indiana. During recess, while floating on the swings, my friend invited me to her house for a sleepover. We would eat junk food, listen to Michael Jackson and Boy George, and tell all the secrets in the world. When got home I made sure my chores and homework were done by the time my father got home. During dinner, I brought up the invitation, already knowing how he normally responded…"You're not a stray dog, you have a home." or "I work hard for you to have a bed and now you just want to leave it." I began by sharing how nice she was and how they might know her parents since they attended mass at our church. My dad listened attentively. He looked up and said he would think about it. As Friday approached I became so anxious. I begged my mom to ask him again. She did and he agreed to let me go as long as I knew I had to be picked up right before everyone went to sleep. I was not happy but since it was the first time he had agreed I took the deal. I couldn't ride the bus like the rest of the girls over to her house. My dad wanted to drop me off. He came to the door, he met her parents. He walked in and asked questions about where they would be and if there were any older brothers around. I was so embarrassed. He then asked what the latest time to pick me up could be. Her mom said as late as I wanted it to be, as long as we were awake. So that night my dad arrived around ten. I remember because my friends looked out the window when they saw the headlights approaching and yelled, "There's your dad!" Again, I was so embarrassed. He must have waited out there a long time. I didn't have to stop having fun. Ultimately, I was tired and her mom walked me out. I said thank you and left. My dad told her that he would bring me back in the morning. He did. At that time my eleven-year-old self-hated it all of it. As I became a mother, I realized I understood his reason behind it. I came to do just about the same. Luckily I have boys and they weren't much for spending the night. When they did, I made sure to meet the parents and at least get to know them a little bit.

A more recent episode was a parent – school conference held about a second-grade student. He was about seven years old. Cute, curious, spontaneous child with little to no evident structure in the home. Parent involvement was a rarity and actually getting a hold of the mother was short of a miracle. The little boy was constantly engaged in breaking school rules, partially, I'm sure he was confident there was no repercussion or follow up at home. The conference was set up because the prior weekend, the seven-year-old and some older middle school and high school students visited the new site to a new school under construction. They tore up some new roofing, broke windows, damaged equipment, and so much more. The police were involved and one of the consequences was to meet with the student and parent in order to give the school district's consequence. During the meeting, the mom was asked if she knew where he had been and she became very irate and loudly yelled to the team about how ridiculous we looked thinking she would know where her seven-year-old was on a Saturday. She told the team that there was no way any parent would know where their elementary school child is all day. Not much was said after that, mostly because I believe all of the educators in the room were in disbelief. Was this parent really trying to stress that parents could not possibly know where their child was on a Saturday? She was absolutely wrong. I think as a parent you are supposed to know where your child is and what they are doing. It is part of being a parent. As young children grow into pre-teens and teenagers, they are absolutely bothered by those type of questions. They would rather we parents knew nothing about their ins and outs. Having raised three boys, I will reiterate and tell you that during those middle school and high school years, it is of utmost importance that you do not sway in your home structure and expectations. Middle school years are some of the most critical years and as parents, we should be more vigilant than ever about our kids. Children in this age bracket are developing both physically but also mentally. They are going through many changes. Do you remember your younger self during middle school years? Hormones are on the loose and sometimes they get in the way of making good decisions.

Summary:

It is very important that we stay connected with our children, including those pre-teen and teenage years. Against their ultimate wishes, we should be consistent in knowing their friends and their activities. It is not going to give you the popular parent award but it will help your child in the long-run see how much you care. (I said the long-run so don't expect anything immediately). Ask lots of questions and let them know you might surprise them and show up just to see them. Again, it will not make you very popular, but your child needs to know you are still the parent and their safety is a top priority.

Here is a tip!

Actually, I think the Google Calendar or any calendar app will go a long way. In addition, make sure you have a couple of their friends' contact information. Be respectful and only use it if it is a definite emergency. I have only had to use it one time. When I could not locate my son because his phone's battery died and my calls went straight to voicemail.

Plant the Seed Well...

You Have Rights

In this chapter, we will venture into:

- Federal Programs that are in place in schools.
- Communicating with your child's school.
- Keeping yourself informed about your school district.

> *"Ask if you don't understand it's your right to know what is happening with your son or daughter.*
> Raul - a dad on Facebook

A repeating question is always about school. Parents have the right to be involved in their child's school. Some of the rights come directly from the U.S. Department of Education ESSA: Every Student Succeeds Act (B. Obama) which replaced NCLB No Child Left Behind (G.Bush). In addition, both local and state taxes are allocated to pay the school system your child attends, therefore everyone from the superintendent to the classroom teacher is paid via the taxes you pay. You have the right to be informed and communicated about policies, practices, and programs. Many schools and school systems have parental involvement policies and programs in place others do not, so it would be up to you to be proactive and seek out information. You have to make it known that you are not only interested in what your child is learning, but the annual goals set forth for your child.

What is Title I?

The Title I Federal Grant is monies awarded to school systems to provide funding in order to improve the academic achievement of the disadvantaged student. It helps balance out any disparities in schools with high numbers or high percentages of children from low-income families to help ensure that all children meet challenging state academic standards. It is awarded to schools and the amount is based on the number of students categorized as living in poverty. There are four different formulas to determine the exact amount each school district or school receives.

Parent Teacher Conferences 101

As a parent, you have the right to request a parent-teacher conference when you feel there's a need. You do not have to wait for a pre-scheduled time frame the school sets for all parents. I scheduled a parent-teacher conference for my three sons every summer right before school started. I remember the first time I scheduled one right before my firstborn was transitioning to middle school. The assistant principal who I had contacted was a bit shocked or confused, maybe both, said, "Well I don't see any record that would give us a reason to meet, he's not had any behavior issues and he is doing very well academically". I responded something like, "I know that, but I need to meet his teachers and would like to hear in a small group setting what their expectations are and for them to hear ours (my husband and I)". Needless to say, she scheduled it, we all met and the transitioning year went as well as expected.

If you ever feel there is a sense that your child needs additional support, you need to meet and ask specifically what type of support is offered. In most cases, local schools are more than happy to support in sharing information that will help them collaborate with parents in ensuring the success of the child. If there is ever a time you feel that's not the case, well then you call the district office. Again, you have rights and after all, everyone has a superior they need to answer to. Since it is a government funded institution there are other federal programs and support systems in place as

FERPA, Title VI, Title IX, IEPs, ESOL and 504 Plans. Let us briefly cover some of these.

FERPA, The Family Educational Rights, and Privacy Act state that parents have the right to inspect and review their child's education records maintained by the school. Parents have the right to request that a school correct records which they believe to be inaccurate. If the school decides not to amend the record, then parents can request a hearing and ultimately they can add a formal letter to add to the record clarifying any errors or misleading information. Last, but not least, FERPA ensures school only provide information from a student's record to anyone else, with parent's written permission. For example, an uncle cannot obtain your child's information unless one of the parents have provided written permission to the school.

Title VI of the Civil Rights Act of 1964 prohibits discrimination based on race, color, or national origin in programs or activities, which receive federal financial assistance, such as schools.

Title IX basically reads, "No person in the United States shall, on

Plant the Seed Well...

the basis of sex, be excluded from participation in, be denied the benefits of, or be subjected to discrimination under any education program or activity receiving Federal financial assistance."

The IEP, *Individualized Educational Plan,* is a plan or program developed to ensure that a child who has a disability identified under the law and is attending an elementary or secondary educational institution receives specialized instruction and related services. In most cases, there's a process that is followed which involves data collection, interventions and lots of communication with parents. You will need to ask lots of questions about what interventions have been implemented to help your child in the regular classroom setting. Once an IEP is written remember you still have rights, you can always deny services, but be very careful and be diligent. An IEP does not mean your child isn't smart, it just means that he/she needs a different type or additional instructional support in order to be successful. There are many things you will need to become knowledgeable about, the school will provide written information and can answer questions during the Eligibility Meeting. One of those important decisions will be whether your child will graduate with a regular education diploma. Another one is whether or not your child will automatically attend summer school. Pay lots of attention and ask lots of questions.

ESOL is a program that supports *English Speakers of Other Languages*. Under both the No Child Left Behind put into place under President George Bush and Elementary and Secondary Education Act under President Barack Obama, there are policies that ensure schools put into place to support limited English speaking students.

504 Plan is a plan developed to ensure that a child who has a medical disability identified under the law and is attending an elementary or secondary educational institution receives accommodations that will ensure their academic success and access to the learning environment. Most schools prefer you bring in medical documentation, but some don't mandate it. So if your child has been diagnosed with ADHD or asthma or even diabetes…share with his/her school. Communication is important.

Sex Education

Plant the Seed Well...

Sex Education or other subjects can be omitted by parents' request to opt out. As a parent, you have to make the request in writing. Each state and local school will have guidelines on how to process these types of requests.

Free Speech

Does my child have free speech rights at school? Yes, but if it disrupts the learning environment it can be banned or paired up with a consequence.

Summary:

We have discussed the importance of communication with your child. The same goes for the school your child attends. You have the right to ask questions, request a parent-teacher conference and learn more about the support your child receives or is eligible for. Parents do not always realize the power of their voice. Schools are funded via local, state and federal funds. Your tax dollars support public education. Federal laws that support education seem to consistently go under a revision process. To keep up with the latest, be sure you are connected with your school district's social media, webpage and that you subscribe to a newsletter via your personal email address.

Here is a tip!

Find out when your next district's board meeting will be held. Board meetings tend to be lengthy, but you will be able to experience the process of voting programs and resources into schools. You will be able to match a face to a name. Learn who your area board member is, note their contact information, again- they work for you.

Plant the Seed Well...

Let Them Fly On Their Own

In this chapter, we will venture into:

- Being positive about the lessons you've instilled in your child and understanding that growth sometimes is challenging.

- Learning how to find a productive use of your "free time".

- Showing support for your young adult even after he/she leaves home.

After what seems to been a life-long 3 Ring Circus… full of extreme chaos, memorable times, and situations that are out of control… you blink and your child is ready to matriculate in a post-secondary quest. Whether it is a pursuit of a college degree, military, or career move the time comes when he/she has to move on and prove to this world that success is the only option.

One of the hardest things to do is letting them go. Trusting that whatever we have taught them will not fail them. To be perfectly transparent, it was definitely not easy for me. All kinds of insecurities arise, was I a good enough parent (great time to reevaluate huh?), did I prepare my child for the uncertainties of the world? Did I instill the real priorities in life, such as happiness and self-love? Did I encourage risk-taking and allowing it to be part of the growth process?

It reminds me a bit of a variation to a grieving process. Here you are, you have had 18 years or so with this child. You have been there for everything from the first steps, first tooth, the first fall off the bike to "Give me your phone" and discussing academic progress when you logged on to the school system to check grades. Now you are supposed to just let them go...well without sounding like a helicopter parent, which by the way you should not be. Everyone grows from falling down and having to get back up on their own. It is healthy for your child to make mistakes and learn from them without your help. At the same time, it is great to set up weekly phone calls, provide reassurance of open-door policy to talk about whatever is happening. In other words, maintain the loving positive relationship with your child. This will help with his/her transition as well as yours. By the way, this would be an excellent time to acquire some type of hobby. As you read this, you know what I chose as mine.

> *"Relax and enjoy, you don't get those days back. Know that they will reach their milestones (potty training, eating with fork and spoon, etc.) in their own time not when you want them too."*
> **Rebecca –a mom on Facebook**

My third and youngest child recently moved out as he begins his next chapter in life. He will be attending a state university and pursuing a degree in Computer Science. I have already encountered this process with my other two cubs (I am Mama Bear). My oldest graduated from college about two years ago. My middle son is a rising junior in college, scheduled to graduate on time like his brother. My youngest will begin his own venture in the Fall. As I reflect on him, I must admit that I have been working on not worrying so much about him. It might be due to the fact that he is the youngest or maybe it has more to do with the "empty nest" syndrome. Either way, I'm taking it one day at a time, reassuring myself that I did the best I could and I work on keeping the communication lines open.

Then there is the possibility of moving back home. It would be unfair to deliberately omit that in the event that your young adult has to move back home you should create a new set of rules. A guideline for a working young adult would be 20% of their monthly check goes to support the household. If he/she is on the search for employment then one job application a day should be submitted and jobs around the house must be on the list. This will help your young adult feel a sense of accountability and responsibility.

Summary:

Your child will not remain young for a long time. They grow up in the blink of an eye. Hard to imagine, but it happens. There is a time to let go and it will be easier if you have been structured and consistent in the relationship you have built with your child. Keep the lines of communication open and continue having high expectations.

Here is a tip!

As your child prepares to leave, write him/her a letter. Let them

Plant the Seed Well...

know how proud you are of the adult they are becoming and also let them know that you will be there for the good times and the bad time. Reassure your young adult that mistakes are bound to happen, but how we react to those mistakes in our lives is what ultimately defines each one of us.

Dedication
Angel

Once upon a time, an angel held my hand,

She wiped away my tears and helped me understand.

Our time on earth is brief, there are lessons to be learned.

She loved me unconditionally, always by my side,

When no one else would listen, in her I could confide.

She saw the light in everyone and gave with no regrets,

Angels come in many forms, for me it was my mother,

Thank you God for giving me the most priceless of all treasures,

I pray that I can someday be everything she hoped I would,

That she is smiling down from heaven knowing she did well.

God's called her to his heavenly home, part of his great plan,

until we meet again my angel.

Written by Nury Castillo Crawford

Plant the Seed Well...

Advice for New Parents

As a parent, if you had to choose one advice to give to new parents, what would it be?

I would like to thank my friends on my social media platforms Facebook, Instagram, Twitter, and LinkedIn who have helped me with this section of the book by contributing their thoughts shared their advice and saw it fit to join in the discussion, ultimately providing advice to new parents.

"Love more, worry less."

Alicia, mom of three on Facebook

"Fully immerse yourself in the moment, cherish every experience!"

Daniel, a dad on Facebook

"Hug them, hold them, and kiss them... a lot! As long as they will let you!"

Heather, a mom on Facebook

"Play!!! And make family traditions!"

Amy, a mom on Facebook

"Pray constantly, about everything and for everything. Engulf your children in love, and let God order your steps as a parent."

Jake, LinkedIn member

"Savour every moment and read to your kids every night."

Courtney, LinkedIn member

"You are your child's primary teacher for the rest of their life."

Gene, LinkedIn member

"I know as parents we want them to be successful and productive... but don't forget to teach them the importance of finding happiness for themselves in this journey... to not wait around for anyone else to make you happy and content."

Vivi, a mom of three boys, on Facebook

"Don't repeat the traumas you were subjected to, assuming you've healed from your own because 'trauma' can be 'transgenerational'."

Rodney, LinkedIn member

"Accept your children's differences. Let them be themselves."

Shannon, a mom on Facebook.

Plant the Seed Well…

Appendix

- Five Reasons You Should be Keeping a Calendar

  cornerstone.edu/blogs/lifelong-learning-matters/post/five-reasons-you-should-be-keeping-a-calendar

- 7 Powerful Tips for Great Parent-Child Communication

  time.com/powerful-tips-for-great-parent-child-communication

- GA Department of Education: Federal Programs

  gadoe.org/School-Improvement/Federal-Programs

Made in the USA
Monee, IL
24 February 2020